POLICE CUSTODY AND HUMAN RIGHT PERSPECTIVE

VOLUME 2, ISSUE 1 OF BRAIN BOOSTER ARTICLES

RADHIKA DWIVEDI

Contents

Preface

"Start writing, no matter what. The water does not flow until the faucet is turned on".

- Louis L'Amour

This book is a bouquet of articles contributed by students, professors and academicians. Hundreds of students and professors are contributing their work to Brain Booster Articles, we are here to provide ample information about Law and Contemporary issues. Our aim is to provide a platform for today's generation to express their views and ideas on law and contemporary law.

CHAPTER ONE

ABSTRACT

In India, since 1999, the National Crime Record Bureau, new Delhi, and the National Human Rights Commission, New Delhi, both under the Home Ministry of the Government of India, have attempted to compile information on specific instances of human rights violations caused by police excesses such as "Illegal Detention", "Fake Encounters", "Extortion", and "Torture". According to the NCRB's 2008 Crime in India Report, 253 incidences of police abuse of human rights were documented throughout the country in 2008. During the year, only 14 police officers were charged and just eight were convicted of these Human Right Violations. According to official data obtained by (TwoCircles.net), every second police encounter in the country is a hoax. State and local officials can routinely meddle with police operations under colonial – era police legislation, sometimes ordering officers to discontinue investigations into people with political ties, including known criminals, and to harass or bring false charges against political opponents. These practises erode public trust.

CHAPTER TWO

INTRODUCTION

On December 10, 1948, the United nations General Assembly overwhelmingly adopted and proclaimed the universe declaration of human right. On 3 January 1976, this universal statement became a legal document known as the international covenant on civil and political rights. On 23rd march 1976, the international covenant on civil and political rights entered into force. India was a signatory to the universal declaration of human right and deposited the instrument of accession to the two international covenants on 10th April 1979. On 25th June 1993, the World Conference on Human Rights adopted the Vienna statement and programme of action, which said that "Human Rights and Fundamental Freedoms are inherent rights of all human beings."

Despite statutory prohibitions against torture and police custodial misconduct, torture is prevalent in police custody and is leading cause of death in detention. The police frequently torture innocent people until they make a "confession" in order to protect powerful and rich culprits.

In 2006, the Supreme Court of India issued seven orders to the federal and state governments to initiate the process of police reform. The primary goals of this series of directives were to provide tenure for and streamline the appointment/ transfer processes for police officers, as well as to increase the police's responsibilities. Human rights are the most fundamental aspect of society and the state, and they encompass a variety of civil, political, social, and cultural rights. However, history records several instances of oppression and arbitrariness perpetrated not just by individuals, but also by authorities or officials of a State. Thus, in carrying out the custody of detainees, the parties in authority must adhere to all legal instruments that formed the foundation for the detention. Without a clear legal foundation for detention, it will devolve into arbitrariness, which is a kind of human rights violation. It is also linked to the Universal

Declaration of Human Rights (UDHR) in Article 5, which states that no one may be tortured or abused, received inhuman treatment or punishment, or having her dignity diminished. The Human Rights Declaration has been incorporated into and incorporated into the principles of common law, and other legislation has adopted it as a requirement to preserve human rights commitments.

The issue of detention is one of the most important in human history because detention itself concerns the value and meaning of, among other things, the deprivation of liberty and freedom of the detained person, the values of humanity and the dignity of humanity, as well as the good name and pollution of the honour personal or he said each detention by itself regarding the limitation and revocation of most human rights.

Since its origin, the law of criminal procedure has been intended to safeguard the public from the arbitrariness of the authorities. As a result, it is sometimes stated that the purpose of criminal procedure legislation is to limit the capacity of the state to act against persons who are participating in the Criminal Procedure Code for detention can be read subjectively by the competent authority.

Custodial Violence is the most severe kind of human rights violation and occurs in police custody. Custodial crimes and torture in police custody are considered heinous and revolting because they reflect a betrayal of custodial trust by public authorities who, despite being tasked with preserving the human rights of defenceless citizens, have turned out to be violators of the same, disregarding the rule of law[1]. The current cases highlight the alarming rate of its increase, which mostly affects the SCs and STs because to their powerlessness and financial backwardness. In 2019, the average number of correctional death was roughly 5 per day. This scenario persists despite national legislation, both substantive and procedural, and many international human rights accords, as well as by weakening the guidelines established by the judiciary over a century ago.

It is also observed that the weaker sectors of society, particularly the SC/ST, are frequently the victims of such brutality. This element is highlighted in the National Commission for SC ST Report, which shows trends in terms of atrocities against them. The law of the land protects them the most in terms of Fundamental Rights, and it was deemed crucial by incorporating it in the Directive Principles of State Policy.

[1]Surekha (ed.) (no date) *A human rights perspective on custodial violence and how the lives of SC/st do not matter, Legal Service India - Law,*

Lawyers and Legal Resources. Available at: https://www.legalserviceindia.com/legal/article-7421-a-human-rights-perspective-on-custodial-violence-and-how-the-lives-of-sc-st-do-not-matter.html (Accessed: October 1, 2022).

CHAPTER THREE

CONCEPT OF HUMAN RIGHTS

As inalienable natural rights, human rights are recognised internationally through a variety of legal instruments. In the beginning, the primary thought of human right was to defend the intrinsic dignity of human individuals and to promote their life and liberty in order to execute justice without deviating from the norms of law. However, in following decades, particularly in the late 1960s and early 1970s, the notion of the common inheritance of mankind has expanded the field of jurisprudential views of human rights to include States and other legal entities. Human rights can be stated as Human Right for All and All for Human Rights, based on the expansionist philosophical concepts of human rights. This definition of human rights include all individuals. This notion of human rights include all individual, including legal people. Internationally, nations are subjects of international law and have entered into different accords to carry out their commitments under municipal law, they operates as protectors of their citizens and all individuals human right. To carry out the UN's vision, the state wouldenforce citizen's rights with the help and cooperation of law enforcement agencies, which might play a critical role in using their powers with proper care and caution.

POWER OF POLICE

The major intention and goal of law in any civilization is to reduce the intensity of disputes and to equip men for the gradual growth of a community. As a result, in order to establish peace and security, the state typically empowers the police to enforce the law and order. As a result, law enforcement officers, particularly police officers, have enormous authorities and tasks. Police, as officers to the state, must enforce their rights in order to prevent crime in society. The law of a sate authorises police to lawfully impose procedures, methods, and means to prevent criminal offences or to locate and apprehend the perpetrators of those offences, as this is the primary mission of police.

<u>CASE LAW</u>

<u>STATE OF HARYANA V BHAJAN AND OTHERS AIR 1992 SC 604</u>

A First Information Report (FIR) was registered by the Haryana Police against Ch Bhajan Lal, on a complaint by a private person that he possessed assets disproportionate to his known sources of income. Bhajan Lal – Union Minister and former Chief Minister of Haryana – went to the High court asking for the FIR to be cancelled, saying that it was registered because of the political rivalry that existed between Ch Devi Lal, the existing Chief Minister of Haryana and him.

The High Court ordered cancellation of the FIR and all proceedings undertaken on its behalf, on the ground that the allegations did not make up a cognizable offence to start a lawful investigation. The State of Haryana appealed to the Supreme Court against the order of the High Court.

<u>TYPES AND FORMS</u>

Section 167 of the CrPC talks about two types of Custody i.e., police custody and judicial custody. Therefore we can divide Custodial violence into two types namely:

<u>VIOLENCE IN POLICE CUSTODY</u>

This type of violence occurs when police torture suspects in order to prolong interrogation and uncover the truth. there are few controls in place to ensure that the individual in custody has prompt access to his lawyer, a record of his confinement, and a proper medical check-up.

VIOLENCE IN JUDICAL CUSTODY

This type of violence is typically witnessed in prisons or detention centres, where it is carried out by convict gangs with unfettered power to do heinous actions. Innocent prisoners are captured by these gangs and assaulted if they do not show allegiance to them. The victim is pushed to commit suicide as a result of this type of violence.

CHAPTER FIVE

FORMS OF CUSTODIAL VIOLENCE

1. <u>**PSYCHOLOGICAL**</u>

It affects the mental stability and composure by using methods such as misleading information, threats, humiliations, or denying the victim of water, food, sleep, and toilet.

1. <u>**PHYSICAL**</u>

It entails creating disfigurement and weariness, as well as torturing the victim to the point that the victim fears quick death.

3. <u>**SEXUAL**</u>

Sexual violence has a social and psychological influence on the victims thinking. It is aimed at the victims dignity.

CHAPTER SIX

HUMAN RIGHTS AND CUSTODIAL VIOLENCE

Human dignity is the highest type of fundamental right, and it is protected even by our Constitution, which is regarded as our country's most important statute book. Article 21 of the Indian constitution provides a person the right to a dignified life and personal liberty. When a person is taken into custody, he or she becomes a legal custody of the state, assuming the guise of legal guardian[1]. All state – run organisations have an obligation to protect them. This concept has been muddled by the activity known as custodial violence, a tendency against human rights and dignity that comes out the perverse impulse to perform such an act when revenge is nearly impossible.

[1]Sinha , A. (no date) *Custodial Violence And Human Rights: Constitutional Perspective, Elementary Education Online.* Available at: https://ilkogretim-online.org/ (Accessed: October 1, 2022).

CHAPTER SEVEN

SUPREME COURT CASES ON THE MATTER

Rudul Shah v. State of Bihar

In this case the petitioner Rudul Shah was kept illegally in jail for 14 years, the writ of habeas corpus was filed and his immediate release was demanded. The court realized for the first time that if any individual's constitutional rights have been violated, then the individual will get compensation.

D.K Basu v. State of West Bengal

In this case, the apex court recognized custodial violence and police torture and said custodial violence is an attack on the human dignity. Court also said after having many recommendations and policies still the cases of torture and deaths in police custody are increasing. So the court issued a list of 11 guidelines that every police officer has to follow while arresting someone.

Nilabati Behera v. State of Orissa

In this case the court observed that every prisoner and the arrestee has the right to enjoy all the fundamental rights and the police have to ensure that they don't deprive the right to life of the prisoner mentioned under article 21. The petitioner Suman Behera was arrested by the police and the very next day her body was found a railway track with multiple injuries, she was awarded a compensation of Rs 1.5 lakh.

ELEMENTS WHICH CONSTITUTE CUSTODIAL VIOLENCE

1. The infection of severe mental physical pain or suffering.
2. By or with the consent or acquiescence of the state authorities.
3. For a specific purposes such as gaining information, punishment or intimation.

PROTECTION UNDER THE CODE OF CRIMINAL PROCEDURE, 1973

The following sections provide the protection under code of criminal procedure, 1973

1. Section 57: It provides that no police officer shall detain in custody a person arrested without warrant for a longer period than under all the circumstances of the case is reasonable and such period shall not, in the absence of a special order of a magistrate under section 167, exceed 24 hours exclusive of the time necessary for the journey from the place of arrest to the court of magistrate.

2. Section 163 provides that :-

- No police officer or other person in authority shall offer or make, or cause to be offered, or make any such inducement, threat or promise as is mentioned in section 24 of Indian Evidence Act.

3. Section 164 provides that:-

- Any such confession shall be recorded in the manner provided in section 281 for recording the examining of an accused person and shall be signed by the person making the confession; and the Magistrate shall make a memorandum at the foot of such record to the following effect.

CHAPTER TEN

NATIONALS LAW GOVERNING CUSTODIAL VIOLENCE IN INDIA

Custodial violence have been dealt with by an array of provisions in national legislation in India. This has been by way of granting few rights to the prisoners / accused / suspect / person while in custody, though there exists no special legislation which deals exclusively with the Custodial violence.

The rights of the accused thus includes the following:

1. Right to Life

One of the basic and fundamental right of the prisoner / suspect /accused person is the right to life. It is conferred by Article 21 of the Constitution of India. The article lays down that a person cannot be deprived of his / her life and personal liberty unless there exists a law, which is enacted by a competent authority that lays down a specific procedure for such deprivation.

Case:- Maneka Gandhi v. UOI

In this case the Supreme court had held that, procedure which is contemplated under Article 21 must be right, just and fair and not arbitrary, fanciful or oppressive, otherwise it would be no procedure at all the requirement of Article 21 would not be satisfied.

2. Right against self – incrimination

The focal point of custodial violence against the accused exists in the interrogation, to extract confession from the suspect for the crime he is alleged to have committed. This has been done so that he confesses the truth. However, the accused has been entrusted with the Fundamental Right to refuse to answer all self – incriminatory questions, under Article 20(3) of the Constitution of India. It is his/her right, not to be compelled to be a witness against himself.

3. Right to be informed of the ground of arrest

The accused is entrusted with the Fundamental Right to be informed on the ground of arrest, in spite of being arrested with or without warrant, under Article 22(1) of Constitution of India. With respect to it, the Supreme Court have also opined that the authorities need not to furnish the full details of the allege offence, but rather, should inform the accused why he has been arrested.

CHAPTER ELEVEN

CONCLUSION

Thus, it can be concluded that, the Custodial Violence is the gravest form of Human Right Violation which act as a blow to the Rule of Law of the Country, as it being committed by the authority which is supposed to be the protector of the rights of the people. Such violation has been committed in the name of official duty of the police to interrogate. The abuse of power by the police is often inflicted upon the marginalised and the poor section of the society. The SC/St community have been victimised for the majority of the custodial violence cases.

The central government should provide financial assistance to modernise the police system in each state so that, they resort to better methods in interrogation which would in turn result in greater efficiency in solving cases before them.